Build a Better Day
For Success

Unleash Your Full Potential
with Daily Motivation
and Positive Affirmations

Lynn Lok-Payne

WELLMINDED
MEDIA

Copyright © 2024 Lynn Lok-Payne

All rights reserved. No portion of this book may be reproduced in any form without permission from the publisher, except as permitted by US copyright law. This book may not be used in any content related to artificial intelligence (AI) without written permission. Any use of this publication to "train" generative artificial intelligence (AI) technologies to generate text is expressly prohibited. The author reserves all rights to license uses of this work for generative AI training and development of machine learning language models.

The information provided within this book is for general informational and educational purposes only and should not be treated as advice. Although the author has made every effort to ensure that the information in this book was correct at press time, the author assumes no responsibility for errors, inaccuracies, omissions, or any other inconsistencies herein and hereby disclaims any liability to any party for any loss, damage, or disruption caused by errors or omissions, whether such errors or omissions result from negligence, accident, or any other cause. Moreover, the author specifically disclaims any implied warranties of merchantability or fitness of use for a particular purpose. Any use of this information is at your own risk.

The medical information in this book is provided with the understanding that the author is not engaged to render any type of medical, psychological, legal, or any other kind of professional advice. If medical, psychological, legal, or other expert assistance is required, the services of a competent professional should be sought. This book does not prescribe or endorse the use of any information, procedure, or exercise as treatment for mental, emotional, physical, or medical problems or issues. Do not substitute this information for the medical advice of physicians. Always consult your doctor for your individual needs. Any action you take upon the information in this book is strictly at your own risk, and the author assumes no responsibility for your actions and will not be liable for any losses and damages in connection with the use of this book.

Library of Congress Control Number: 2023922915

ISBN: 9781736459751 (hardback), 9781736459744 (paperback), 9781736459737 (ebook)

Published by WellMinded Media
3941 Park Drive, Ste 20-559, El Dorado Hills, CA 95762

www.LynnLokPayne.com
Designed by McKenna Payne
Printed in The United States of America
First Edition: 2024
1 2 3 4 5 6 7 8 9 10

I dedicate this book to the brave ones
who choose to improve themselves
and build better lives every day.

And to my daughter, McKenna,
who helped build a better book
and taught me the true meaning
of a successful human.

Contents

PREFACE: What is Success?   VII

1. Success Starts Here   1
2. Create Goals   19
3. Build Better Habits   49
4. Develop a Growth Mindset   71
5. Don't Give Up   93
6. The Qualities of Leadership   115
7. Dream Big   133
8. Live Your Legacy   153

APPENDIX

Playlist for Success   165
Thank You   167
Notes   169
Index   175

What is Success?

What is success? Everyone's definition is different. Whether it's a great relationship, a fulfilling career, a beautiful home, pure happiness, peaceful abundance, or a combination of things, many of us search for success outside of ourselves. But we will not find it "out there." True success lives within—it's how we feel about ourselves and our lives. If we aren't living the lives we love, then it is up to us to change what is necessary.

In today's hectic world, with so many personal and business demands, from emails and social media to meetings and events, we rarely make enough time for personal growth. We focus on external and seemingly urgent issues instead of taking important steps to nurture our aspirations and well-being.

That's why I wrote this book. To inspire people to prioritize their dreams and give them a framework to focus, create a plan, and take action toward living the lives they want.

Build a Better Day For Success is organized into eight chapters including Success Starts Here, Create Goals, Build Better Habits, Develop a Growth Mindset, Don't Give Up, The Qualities of Leadership, Dream Big, and Live Your Legacy. Each page starts with a positive affirmation, followed by simple ideas and motivational quotes to help elevate your day and improve your life. Just making consistent 1% daily changes can lead to full transformation.

This book is designed like a road map, giving you the directions to guide you throughout the turns and detours in your journey to success. However, start wherever you feel called to embark, or simply open the book to any page and let that be your inspirational message for the day.

Build a Better Day For Success encourages you to:
- Harness the power of positive affirmations to improve your self-talk
- Supercharge your daily routine by incorporating inspirational quotes for motivation
- Make yourself a top priority and maximize your potential
- Cultivate a growth mindset to transform your dreams into reality
- Break free from your comfort zone and embrace a life you truly love

By incorporating the tips in this book into our daily routines, we can define success on our own terms and create the lives we desire. Whatever we are searching for is within our grasps. It all begins with building a better day!

"It's never too late to be what you might have been."

— GEORGE ELIOT

1

Success Starts Here

"What is your idea of success? Not what your family, friends, or society expects of you. What is your definition? Once you decide, chase it."

— LYNN LOK-PAYNE

BUILD A BETTER DAY FOR SUCCESS

I have the power to make my dreams a reality.

What have you always wanted to do or accomplish? What does it look like? How would you feel if you were to achieve it? Every day, spend a little time visualizing yourself already living this life. Imagine and believe it, create a strategy, and then put it into motion. Be bold and be brave.

Takeaway: The power to manifest your dreams lies within you, through inspiration, belief, desire, and action.

> "The surest way to make your dreams come true is to live them."
> — ROY T. BENNETT

SUCCESS STARTS HERE

I can do this!

Taking action is necessary if we desire something. This applies to every single area of our lives. In order to enter college or start a new job, we fill out an application. To make a sale or gain a client, we initiate a connection. To construct a building, it's essential we launch with a blueprint. It all starts with action.

Takeaway: Every goal that is worth pursuing begins with making the first move.

> "A journey of a thousand miles begins with a single step."
> — **CHINESE PROVERB**

I have faith in myself.

Before we begin our goals, we would like to see the full map of the journey. We want evidence of our potential success to make sure that the use of our energy and time is worth the investment.

However, we really just need to see the first step. We have to believe that the journey will lead us closer to our dreams coming true.

Takeaway: Have faith in yourself because in order for your dreams to become reality, you need to begin.

> "Take the first step in faith. You don't have to see the whole staircase, just take the first step."
> — MARTIN LUTHER KING JR.

SUCCESS STARTS HERE

I will begin now.

The beginning is where every person on the road to success starts. People don't build a company or an empire overnight. Leaders may impress us with their wisdom, but they didn't possess this knowledge at first; they gained it over time. They probably had a limited understanding of their job or industry. However, they kept trying, failing, and learning. This is how they became leaders; they kept persevering.

Takeaway: All success has a starting point.

> "You don't have to be great to start,
> but you have to start to be great."
>
> — ZIG ZIGLAR

If they can do it, then I can, too.

You gain insight by observing successful people. If you want to thrive in a certain industry, research its leaders. Find out what actions they took, how they did it, and why. The 'why' could be the motivation behind their success. Follow the trail, learn their steps, take what resonates with you, and disregard the rest. Use others as an inspiration, but create the path that's right for you.

Takeaway: Other people's successes offer proof that the path is possible.

> "Success leaves clues. Go figure out what someone who was successful did, and model it. Improve it, but learn their steps. They have knowledge."
>
> — TONY ROBBINS

SUCCESS STARTS HERE

I release the beliefs that no longer serve me.

Ask yourself, "Why not me instead of someone else?" Let go of your limiting beliefs. It doesn't matter what your life was before this moment. You have the power to change your present circumstances and improve your future.

Be your own coach and start training to make the goal. Get in the game and be the MVP in your life. Somebody has to be on the podium to collect the trophy. Why not you?

Takeaway: You gear up for game-changing shifts when you drop your limiting beliefs. This one step alone will have a profound impact on your life.

> "We like to think of our champions and idols
> as superheroes who were born different from us.
> We don't like to think of them as relatively ordinary people
> who made themselves extraordinary."
> — CAROL DWECK

What I need to succeed will appear once I start.

There has never been a better time than right now to launch your dream life. Don't wait to finish your to-do list before you begin because as soon as you complete one item, another will appear. I've discovered that there will always be more to do, so prioritize your dreams. Don't hesitate.

And if someone says to you, "It's not the right time," or "The conditions are just too hard right now," it's because they're not working toward their own goals. Challenging times can be a great opportunity to launch something new because there's less competition. What matters is not how many resources you have; it's how well you utilize them.

Takeaway: Don't put off your dreams waiting for everything to line up. If it's important to you, begin now.

> "Do not wait; the time will never be 'just right.' Start where you stand, and work with whatever tools you may have at you command, and better tools will be found as you go along."
> — **NAPOLEON HILL**

SUCCESS STARTS HERE

Today is the day
I get into the game!

We all know the adage, "You miss 100% of the shots you don't take." Often, we convince ourselves that scoring is impossible, so we don't bother trying. But what does impossible mean? It's just a belief we created. It doesn't mean it's true. We are the ones who get to decide what's possible and what's not.

Stop sitting on the sidelines watching life pass you by. Start showing up and playing. It's how you achieve success. Seize the moment. Take your shot now.

Takeaway: I must play to win.

"You can't win the game if you don't even play it."
— ROBIN SHARMA

Now is the time for me to act.

Action is necessary for progress. Our true potential will remain unknown if we don't begin. Yes, there will be mistakes, disappointments, and defeat. The road to success is filled with wrong turns and detours. Perhaps the side trip had a purpose, even if it's a lesson in what not to do. This is the learning curve. Its purpose is to help us create a better path for ourselves. Starting is essential to unlocking our happiness and potential.

Takeaway: Satisfied + action = satis*faction*.

"If you don't take action, you fail by default."
— LYNN LOK-PAYNE

SUCCESS STARTS HERE

I trust that my intuition will lead the way.

We have to believe that our instincts will steer us in the right direction. Too often, fear and self-doubt hold us back. It's okay not to have all the answers. Solutions will emerge. Trust the process.

Other times, we believe we're not worthy or capable of fulfilling our desires. *But we are.* The resources to achieve our goals will appear once we embark on our dreams. Have faith that it will all work out in the end.

Takeaway: The universe is always working in our favor.

> "You can't connect the dots looking forward;
> you can only connect them looking backward.
> So, you have to trust that the dots will somehow connect
> in your future. You have to trust in something—
> your gut, destiny, life, karma, whatever.
> This approach has never let me down,
> and it has made all the difference in my life."
>
> — STEVE JOBS

I visualize my success every day.

Picture your goal or dream as if it's already come true. What does success look like—a balanced routine, healthy relationships, a certain lifestyle, financial stability, or great health? How does it make you feel—happy, capable, valued, powerful, proud, or free? Embody the feeling of success and watch the transformation begin.

Takeaway: Visualization is like any muscle. The more you use it, the more powerful it becomes.

> "Visualize what you want to do before you do it. Visualization is so powerful that when you know what you want, you will get it."
>
> — AUDREY FLACK

SUCCESS STARTS HERE

It's up to me to change my life.

We alone hold the responsibility for the outcome of our lives. It's up to us to shape or reinvent ourselves. When we get clear about our wants and who we aspire to be, serendipity steps in and connects us with people, places, and inspiration to help.

Takeaway: The journey begins with you.

> "The self is made, not given."
> — BARBARA MYERHOFF

What am I waiting for?

We may look back a month, a year, or a lifetime from now and ask ourselves, "Why did I not start earlier?" In hindsight, the things we don't do and the chances we didn't take often lead to regret. Achieving our dreams requires leaving the safety of our comfort zones.

To have something different, we have to do something different. We do this by letting go of the old things that no longer serve us and redirecting ourselves toward something new. If we fail, at least we tried. What if failure paves the way for something even more amazing than what we initially dreamt of?

Takeaway: It's often better to have tried than regret the actions I didn't take.

> "A year from now you may wish you had started today."
> — KAREN LAMB

SUCCESS STARTS HERE

I won't allow my mind's rumination to control my life.

Break the belief that says, "I can't do it." Sometimes we need to be brave, take the plunge, and just go. No one knows everything in the beginning. We must leap to find out.

Takeaway: Push off without delay.

> "You can't be that kid standing at the top of the water slide overthinking it. You have to go down the chute."
> — TINA FEY

Taking small steps will help me reach my dreams.

Making one move today and building on it tomorrow sets the wheel in motion. All actions have a purpose and no piece is too minor. For example, lug nuts may be tiny, however they play a vital role—they secure the tire to the vehicle, allowing it to move.

Small steps are always necessary to build the foundation for what comes next, and from there, we create momentum. Eventually, we will get to where we are living what we once only dreamt of.

Takeaway: Audrey Hepburn said it best, "Nothing is impossible. The word itself says 'I'm Possible'!"

> "Start by doing what's necessary; then do what's possible; and suddenly you are doing the impossible."
> — ST. FRANCIS OF ASSISI

SUCCESS STARTS HERE

My motivation increases when I honor all of my wins.

Celebrate your progress. Acknowledge, honor, and applaud the mini milestones because they will bring in more inspiration and courage to go the distance. Embrace the lessons along the way because they can make you stronger, more determined. And give your attention to the experiences that occur in your daily life. This is where you spend most of your time—in the miraculous ordinary moments.

Make the first move. Revel in it and all the steps that follow. Let's go!

Takeaway: Celebrating and savoring the adventures of life makes the journey worthwhile.

> "Remember to celebrate milestones as you prepare for the road ahead."
> — NELSON MANDELA

2

Create Goals

"I am able to achieve what I can conceive."

— LYNN LOK-PAYNE

I set goals that align with my dreams.

If you can dream it, believe it, and act on it, success is achievable. Navigate your dream journey starting with these four steps.

- Define your dream. *What do I want?*
- Identify the reason. *Why do I want it?*
- Make the choice to chase your dream. *What decision can I make?*
- Commit to the work. *Am I willing to do what it takes to achieve it?*

Takeaway: When desire, conviction, and action align, I become unstoppable.

> "A goal is just a dream that you bring into reality."
>
> — LYNN LOK-PAYNE

CREATE GOALS

I have unlimited potential and endless possibilities.

Your mind believes what it is told, so tell it good things. There's nothing stopping you from creating your dreams except doubt or fear. Just because you think something doesn't make it true. This was an aha moment for me—that my thoughts may not hold the truth. Your dreams and self-belief are vital to manifesting your goals. Have confidence and come up with a plan.

Takeaway: Goals are tools for manifestation.

> "Setting goals is the first step in turning the invisible into the visible."
> — TONY ROBBINS

I devise a game plan for my success.

Without clear focus, we'll end up running in many directions and lose our way. Football players don't move the ball down the field without a play. First, they begin with a game plan. Kick-start your life with a well-planned goal.

Takeaway: Strategize for the win.

> "The trouble with not having a goal is that you can spend your life running up and down the field and never score."
> — BILL COPELAND

CREATE GOALS

My desire is the foundation of my inspiration.

What do you desire? Once you decide, outline the initial tasks. What's your first step? What tools or skills are necessary? How are you going to achieve it? When do you want to complete it by? Set aside time for your goal every day, even if it's just 15 or 30 minutes. Once you begin, watch as inspiration unfolds.

Takeaway: Desire is essential to achieving your goals.

"The starting point of all achievement is desire."
— NAPOLEON HILL

I can reverse engineer my dream life.

Begin with the end goal, then break it down into small steps by working backward. If you want a promotion at work or to launch your own business, what small action can you do today? Below are some examples:

- Enroll in a class
- Read a personal development book
- Research how to start a business
- Create a business plan
- Apply for a business license
- Open a business checking account
- Get a URL
- Launch a side hustle

Today is the day to start living your dreams.

Takeaway: Start by envisioning your future and work backward to determine the steps.

> "Instead of looking at the past,
> I put myself ahead twenty years
> and try to look at what I need to do now
> in order to get there then."
> — DIANA ROSS

CREATE GOALS

Action is necessary to achieve my dreams.

A goal is just a dream more defined. What dreams do you want to achieve?

Takeaway: Line up your actions to your dreams.

> "When dreams and actions collide, success cannot help but follow."
> — LYNN LOK-PAYNE

I can reach my goals by breaking them down into manageable steps.

SMART goals are specific, measurable, achievable, relevant, and timely.[1]

- Specific: What is it I want to achieve? Be specific.
- Measurable: What metrics can I use to track my progress and measure success?
- Achievable: Is it realistic?
- Relevant: Does this goal align with my dreams and values?
- Time-Bound: When is the completion date?

The answers to these questions will help determine the feasibility of the goal and provide a blueprint for achieving it.

Takeaway: It's not just the plan that matters; it's how well it's executed that determines success.

> "A dream written down with a date becomes a goal.
> A goal broken down into steps becomes a plan.
> A plan backed by action makes your dreams come true."
> — GREG S. REID

CREATE GOALS

My goals create the target for my success.

Be *specific* when setting goals. If you want to increase your knowledge, make it a goal to read about a topic for one hour every night at eight in your favorite chair. You'll hit nothing without a clear target.

If it's important, then make it a goal. Any area in life—career, relationships, personal development, money, travel, or spiritual connection—can be transformed by setting goals.

Takeaway: Clear goals lead us to our desired destination.

> "If you aim at nothing, you will hit it every time."
> — ZIG ZIGLAR

BUILD A BETTER DAY FOR SUCCESS

Every day I show up for myself and dedicate my time to doing what is necessary.

Measurable goals are motivating because they provide built-in milestones to guide and track your progress. A clear and quantifiable goal encourages action.

To illustrate, imagine you want to buy a house in three years and the required down payment is $20K. If you divide $20K by 36 months, you get a monthly savings goal of $555. You could break it down even further to about $129 per week or $19 per day in savings. These numbers are much less intimidating than $20K.

Measurable objectives help you to have a direct focus, know when you're reaching your goals, and celebrate your wins along the way.

Takeaway: Benchmarks are an instrument to guide and measure success.

> "People with goals succeed because they know where they're going."
> — EARL NIGHTINGALE

CREATE GOALS

I set realistic goals that challenge and engage me.

Achievable goals should push us beyond our comfort zones, but not so much that we quickly get overwhelmed and quit. Feeling that they are attainable is essential to giving our best effort.

By breaking our goals down into smaller steps and focusing on one action at a time, we reduce the pressure we put on ourselves and make our dreams feel within reach.

Takeaway: Achievable goals set the attitude for success.

> "The goal you set must be challenging.
> At the same time, it should be realistic and attainable, not impossible to reach. It should be challenging enough to make you stretch, but not so far that you break."
> — RICK HANSEN

Understanding my 'why' gives me the purpose to pursue my goals.

Are our goals *relevant* to the lives we want to create? Goals give us direction and it's essential to understand the underlying motivation behind them. The emotion behind our why holds more power than our rational thoughts. For example, if getting up early is a goal, but staying in bed feels better, our emotions can override the goal. Or if our goal is to increase our income, but we don't have an important why, then how can we achieve meaningful success?

Assigning a why allows us to establish more fulfilling objectives. In the previous income example, what we may truly desire is not the money itself—it's the freedom that money can provide to create the life experiences we want. Dig deep to find your why.

Goals that serve a purposeful why inspire us to act. They give us the understanding of what we're truly reaching for, the underlying motivation, and the inspiration to manifest our dreams.

Takeaway: Build goals based on your why. It's a powerful motivator.

CREATE GOALS

"Goals give you that sense of meaning and purpose, a clear sense of direction. As you move toward your goals you feel happier and stronger. You feel more energized and effective. You feel more competent and confident in yourself and your abilities."

— BRIAN TRACY

When I establish a timeline, I can reach my dreams.

Timelines and *time-bound* goals ensure accountability and provide the motivation needed to stay on track. If you want to run a 5K in two months, it's necessary to set a daily training schedule. If your goal is to launch a new business in six months, make a task list with a timetable. Craft a strategy, adapt as needed, and celebrate the mini achievements.

Takeaway: Create a realistic time frame.

> "A goal without a timeline is just a dream."
> — ROBERT HERJAVEC

CREATE GOALS

My focus is not just on the end goal, but also on my own growth journey.

When we solely focus on just the destination, we miss so much of the journey—lessons, knowledge, inspiration, and people we meet along the way. These are the invaluable experiences and moments that make the adventure so extraordinary.

Enjoy the process because today is the only power we have. It's where we find our happiness, confidence, and strength. Remember that we've achieved something simply by going for it.

Takeaway: The experiences we gather during the journey are often worth more than the destination itself.

> "What you get by achieving your goals is not as important as what you become by achieving your goals."
>
> — ZIG ZIGLAR

BUILD A BETTER DAY FOR SUCCESS

Commitment to my goal is paramount to success.

This is where most of us fail in achieving what we want—we don't stick to our goals. The road gets hard, we hit an obstacle, or a challenge surfaces, so we give up. Our doubt, fear, and negative self-talk reveal our insecurities, so we don't continue. Or someone tells us it's impossible, so we stop trying. Setbacks are inevitable. Everyone has them.

Here's what you should know: staying dedicated to your goals will make you feel more capable because you start building the belief that you can achieve the things you desire. This improves confidence, productivity, and performance. Commit to your goals and you'll succeed.

Takeaway: Commitment changes everything.

> "This one step: choosing a goal and sticking to it, changes everything."
>
> **— SCOTT REED**

CREATE GOALS

I concentrate on my own goals, not on what others are thinking or doing.

When we focus on others' performances and opinions, we lose sight of our goals. Comparison is a no-win situation and can manipulate our mindset, making us question our worth and abilities. When we eliminate the internal chatter of comparison, we can focus on our plan. Don't worry about what everyone else is doing. Follow your purpose.

Takeaway: Focus on your own strengths and goals.

> "I don't focus on what I'm up against.
> I focus on my goals and I try to ignore the rest."
> — VENUS WILLIAMS

I follow my own desires and dreams.

It's inspiring to hear of other people's success stories, however, you don't need to strictly follow their paths. You have your own dreams waiting to be fulfilled. Draw inspiration from others, but set your own personal goals. What are you deeply passionate about? What lights you up? Search within and determine what matters the most to you.

Takeaway: You'll create a life that feels authentic by following your own plan.

> "Each of you, as an individual, must pick your own goals. Listen to others, but do not become a blind follower."
> — THURGOOD MARSHALL

CREATE GOALS

Success is living my purpose.

Purpose lies within our desires. It's the reason we get up in the morning and what motivates us to persist, even in the face of adversity. Decisions based on purpose feel right because they reflect our values. It brings meaning to our lives, and gives clarity on what we want and don't want. When we know our purpose, we can stay strong and refuse to compromise on our non-negotiables. There are no right or wrong answers. Everyone has their own unique purpose.

Takeaway: Your desires hold the key to your purpose.

> "Desire is the factor that determines what your definite purpose in life shall be."
> — NAPOLEON HILL

I am more driven to keep going when I align my passions with my purpose.

Goals backed by passion and purpose have more impact. When you live and build your purpose, often you don't have to look for inspiration and motivation—it's already burning inside of you. Purpose is a feeling of "I must do this" because the desire is too great. Even when you hit challenges, you'll pick yourself up and keep moving. Collaborate with this passion and experience the benefits of fulfillment, happiness, and peace.

Takeaway: Passion is the emotional driver to discover your purpose.

> "When I align my passions to my purpose, my motivation skyrockets."
> — LYNN LOK-PAYNE

CREATE GOALS

I design my destiny.

The truth in the quote below is undeniable. However, that doesn't imply that you should start your own business. You can pursue your own goals while working for someone else. If your intent is to get a college degree or be able to pick your kids up from school, then seek a job with a flexible schedule that allows you to achieve these objectives. Follow your dream.

Takeaway: Don't let someone else's plans overshadow your own. Create a life that works for you.

> "If you don't have big dreams and goals,
> you'll end up working for someone that does."
>
> — UNKNOWN

I am aware of the power within me.

At times, we surrender our power to something beyond ourselves. We may believe others have more knowledge, so we give them our power. Or we convince ourselves that we are powerless in changing our circumstances.

Our strength lies in how we choose to act and react in a situation. We always have a choice and that is the root of our power.

Takeaway: Trust in your abilities and stand tall in your power.

> "The most common way people give up their power is by thinking they don't have any."
> — ALICE WALKER

CREATE GOALS

I adapt to achieve my goal.

Keep in mind that a plan isn't static; we can adjust it. Just because we hit a wall doesn't mean that the goal isn't attainable. We can change our approach.

Takeaway: Keep refining until it works.

> "When it is obvious that the goals cannot be reached, don't adjust the goals, adjust the action steps."
> — CONFUCIUS

I prioritize the important tasks and delegate or delete the rest.

The Eisenhower Decision Matrix is a valuable tool for prioritizing tasks.[2] It's divided into four quadrants—important & urgent, important & not urgent, not important & urgent, and not important & not urgent. I've noticed that urgent matters are often others' demands. Check the chart to get focused and conquer your to-do list.

THE EISENHOWER DECISION MATRIX[3]

Here's how to prioritize and tackle your tasks:
1. First, do what is important and urgent.
2. Next, schedule what is important and not urgent.

CREATE GOALS

3. Then, delegate what is not important, but urgent.
4. Finally, delete what is not important and not urgent.

Takeaway: Focus on important tasks.

> "I am constantly re-evaluating my goals and trying to strike items from my to-do list that aren't critical."
> — AISHA TYLER

BUILD A BETTER DAY FOR SUCCESS

I am in charge of my life.

Most people are too focused on their own goals to take yours into consideration. Design a plan that feels purposeful and authentic to you. This doesn't mean that you won't help other people work on their goals from time to time because life is about collaboration. Just don't let someone else plan your life.

Takeaway: The power to change your life is within your own hands.

> "If you don't design your own life plan, chances are you'll fall into someone else's plan. And guess what they have planned for you? Not much."
> — JIM ROHN

CREATE GOALS

I release my limiting beliefs and embrace possibility.

What beliefs are holding you back from success? I'm not smart enough, I'm not thin enough, I'm too old, I don't have the proper education or money, I can't do it, and the list goes on. Many of these limiting thoughts are not based on truth. Revise anything that starts with "I can't," "I'm not," or "I don't."

Free yourself from negative thoughts and embrace empowering beliefs. Your potential is greater than you realize. You are worthy, capable, and intelligent. You can succeed!

Takeaway: With true belief, we can accomplish amazing feats.

> "You are never too old to set another goal or to dream a new dream."
> — C. S. LEWIS

I can achieve my goals when I commit to the work.

Four Steps to Manifest Your Dreams:
1. Decide what dreams are important to you.
2. Uncover the 'why' behind your dreams.
3. Set goals and break them down into manageable steps.
4. Commit to the work, act, and maintain momentum.
5. Bonus: Adjust as needed.

Actions turn possibilities into probabilities. However, sometimes you'll start a goal to find out it's not worth pursuing. That's okay; it's part of the process. Be flexible and you may discover a more suitable option. When your dreams and actions align, you create your best life.

Takeaway: Make a personal vow to pursue your dreams.

> "Dream it's possible. Then plan, focus, execute. The result will be you living your dream."
> — LYNN LOK-PAYNE

3
Build Better Habits

"It's a chain of influence: actions create habits, habits shape days, and days determine our lives."

— LYNN LOK-PAYNE

BUILD A BETTER DAY FOR SUCCESS

My success depends on my daily habits.

Successful people work at being successful. Their daily routines and habits keep them on track to reach their goals. Consistency is what gets them to the finish line.

Visual prompts help build consistent habits. Create cues, like laying out exercise clothes the night before or leaving a gratitude journal on the nightstand.

Takeaway: Our daily practices determine our levels of success.

> "Success is the sum of small efforts, repeated day-in and day-out."
> — ROBERT COLLIER

BUILD BETTER HABITS

I am in control of my day.

To achieve goals in all areas of your life, create productive habits including self-care and self-development. These areas often get neglected. Carve out time daily or weekly for exercise, meditation, relaxation, reading, learning, or connecting with like-minded people. Seek personal growth to help you reach your goals.

Takeaway: Schedule time for personal care and development.

> "You'll never change your life
> until you change something you do daily.
> The secret of your success is found
> in your daily routine."
> — JOHN C. MAXWELL

I will replace my bad habits by creating more empowering ones.

Whether or not we realize it, we become our habits. They influence who we are, what we do, and how we think. If we desire change, we must create it. Otherwise, we become spectators rather than participants in life.

Takeaway: Do we allow our habits to control us or do we control our habits?

> "First we form habits, then they form us. Conquer your bad habits or they will conquer you."
> — ROB GILBERT

BUILD BETTER HABITS

I am mindful of how I allocate my time.

Behaviors we consistently practice will eventually become automatic, like walking, driving, or riding a bike. Research has shown around 40% of our habits are unconscious, meaning we're often moving on autopilot.[4] If we want to change our habits, we have to consciously replace them with different ones.

Takeaway: Daily habits determine future success.

> "The best preparation for tomorrow is doing your best today."
> — H. JACKSON BROWN, JR.

I can build new habits by noticing my daily patterns.

All habits share the same fundamental steps. This neurological loop consists of a cue, a routine, and a reward, as discovered by MIT researchers.[5] As an example, let's take the scenario of preparing coffee.

- Cue: You walk into the kitchen and see your coffee maker.
- Routine: You insert the coffee grounds or a coffee pod into the machine.
- Reward: You feel the caffeine boost.

If the reward is enjoyable, you'll most likely restart the process the next day. Establishing habits relies on the repeated execution of this pattern.

Takeaway: By understanding how we form habits, we have the power to transform our lives.

> "The brain is so malleable, we can make our own pattern generators."
> — ANN GRAYBIEL

Each day, I have the opportunity to change my life through my actions.

In *Atomic Habits* by James Clear, he adds another layer to the habits loop: cue, *craving*, response, and reward.[6] Craving is not the reward itself; it's the anticipation of the reward. This anticipation leads to a rise in dopamine, which is one of the brain's happy chemicals, and drives us to act.[7]

In the previous coffee example, the craving could be imagining the joy of holding a warm beverage or expecting an exciting energy boost. It's important to note that what we are craving is not the thing itself; it's the feeling that it will give us.

Takeaway: Make the choice to cultivate better habits.

> "Every action you take is a vote for the person you wish to become."
> — JAMES CLEAR

When I stack my habits, implementing new practices becomes easier.

Habit stacking is combining an old habit with a new one. Take a routine task like brushing your teeth. Now add something new, such as reading affirmations or drinking a glass of water after you brush. Or if you watch TV, take advantage of commercial breaks to get up and move. This method is a wonderful strategy for building a new practice by integrating it with an existing one.

Stacking habits is based on *Tiny Habits* by BJ Fong, who runs the Behavior Design Lab at Stanford. He says the key is to make your habits super tiny and super easy.[8] Here is his formula for developing new habits.

Tiny Habits Formula:[9]
- After I… (Do the existing habit that will remind you to do your new one.)
- I will… (Insert new habit.)
- Then I'll celebrate. (Create a positive feeling of accomplishment.)

Takeaway: Habit stacking improves the success of adopting a new behavior.

BUILD BETTER HABITS

"Habit stacking works because you eliminate the stress of adding too many new things to your life. Instead, you begin with a few simple but effective habits and then build on them as this routine becomes an important 'can't miss' part of your day."

— S.J. SCOTT

BUILD A BETTER DAY FOR SUCCESS

My morning habits create the groundwork for my day.

Be intentional in your morning routine. Begin with self-care activities like reading, meditating, journaling, exercising, etc. Setting up my mornings for success has made me more productive. Kick-starting my day with an activity I love brings me more balance and grounding.

Start the day unplugged. When you dive into technology first, it can lead to getting absorbed in articles, experiencing stressful emails, or spending too much time on social media when you only meant to check in.

"Research has shown that a consistent morning routine can reduce stress, boost your energy levels and improve your productivity at work."[10] Do what's important to you. Unimportant matters can usually be dealt with later in the day. Get your morning off on the right foot.

Takeaway: Having an effective morning routine can boost productivity and confidence, while minimizing stress.

> "Morning is an important time of day because how you spend your morning can often tell you what kind of day you are going to have."
> — LEMONY SNICKET

BUILD BETTER HABITS

I align my habits to be in sync with my dreams and goals.

Achieving dreams requires developing productive habits, which are the building blocks to manifesting desires. When dreams and habits are not in harmony, achieving what you want becomes more difficult, if not impossible.

Takeaway: Success increases when habits align with dreams.

> "If your habits don't line up with your dream, then you need to either change your habits or change your dream."
> — JOHN C. MAXWELL

BUILD A BETTER DAY FOR SUCCESS

I practice habits that lead me in the right direction.

According to one study, it takes about 66 days on average to form a habit, so don't quit.[11] Take small steps and let your successes fuel your perseverance. Remember why you're striving for this goal. There might be instances where you slip back into an old habit or fail to practice the new one. Just try again. Don't doubt yourself, you can do this!

Takeaway: Be patient. Forming a new habit takes time.

> "Motivation is what gets you started.
> Habit is what keeps you going."
> — JIM ROHN

With small steps, I can transform my habits.

Research shows we don't erase habits—they live in our brains until they're replaced with new ones.[12] If you're struggling to let go of a habit, try transforming it through incremental changes.

For example, if you want to swap the daily habit of drinking soda with a healthier alternative, replace it with seltzer water mixed with juice. Once the habit of drinking seltzer and juice is established, switch to sparkling water with lemon. Ensure that each change moves you closer to your goal.

Progress starts with baby steps, which eventually lead to larger ones. Even small wins provide a dopamine kick, keeping you motivated.

Takeaway: My strength lies in my ability to exchange a habit with a more beneficial one.

> "The Golden Rule of Habit Change:
> You can't extinguish a bad habit, you can only change it."
> — **CHARLES DUHIGG**

When I know the reason and emotion behind a habit, it becomes easier to change.

As we discussed in the last chapter, our 'why' is powerful. Let's say I wonder why I stay up late when I clearly need more sleep. Am I experiencing stress, loneliness, or a desire for comfort or excitement? By acknowledging these feelings, I can adjust and improve my habits.

Takeaway: Identifying and understanding emotions will help to change behavior.

> "The 'why' emotion behind a habit is a powerful motivator."
> — LYNN LOK-PAYNE

BUILD BETTER HABITS

I will step into my power by choosing to uplift my thoughts.

Notice your internal dialogue. What is being said? Is your self-talk supporting you or bringing you down? Turn negative chatter into something empowering. Instead of saying, "I need to," "I must," or "I should," reframe it to, "I get to," "I can," or "I could." Highlight the upside, not the downside.

We can get so wrapped up in our pessimistic thoughts that we abandon our dreams. Worry is natural because our brains have a negativity bias, meaning they're programmed to find potential problems and prevent them for our survival. But when we become aware our thinking, we can change it. Revise the negative to something more beneficial.

Takeaway: Your mindset shapes your reality.

> "One habit overlooked is mindset.
> Your mind repeats the same thoughts and beliefs.
> To create a new mindset, become aware of your thinking.
> What you think and believe on a daily basis
> is the key to your success."
> — LYNN LOK-PAYNE

I will find a reason to be grateful every day.

Our brains are like computers—we act based on our programming. And once habits are hard-wired into the brain, we do these tasks automatically. This includes our thinking.

Both pessimism and optimism are habits. We can improve our mindset by infusing our daily routines with positive thoughts and gratitude. To foster optimism, focus on the good, spend time with upbeat people, and don't listen to the cynics. With practice, our gratitude list can expand.

Takeaway: Prioritizing gratitude paves the way for success.

"Positivity is like a muscle: keep exercising it, and it becomes a habit."

— NATALIE MASSENET

BUILD BETTER HABITS

Today, I stop making excuses and begin working on my dreams.

Pursuing our dreams is often hindered by our excuses. They shift personal responsibility to something we perceive as beyond our control. These are just fears or doubts masquerading as "valid reasons" for our inaction. I've experienced these firsthand.

I once shared with a friend a list of reasons why I couldn't find time to exercise. When she called me out and said, "Sounds like a list of excuses," I realized I wasn't taking responsibility for my actions.

Break down the excuses, pinpoint the underlying fears or doubts, and devise strategies to overcome or address them.

Takeaway: Drop the excuses and don't dwell on why it's not possible; instead, strive for progress.

> "Success occurs when your dreams are bigger than your excuses."
> — UNKNOWN

I refuse to let my excuses prevent me from achieving my goals.

Six Steps to Drop Excuses:
1. Take ownership of your actions.
2. Are you explaining why you're unable to do something? If so, it might be an excuse. You don't need to justify yourself to anyone.
3. Embrace uncertainty. It's alright to not have all the answers.
4. Avoid comparison and procrastination. Neither is beneficial to living your best life.
5. Replace excuses with action. For instance, if you're too busy to exercise, start with just five to ten minutes a day until it becomes a habit.
6. Create clear and realistic goals. Craft a plan, breaking it down into manageable steps and habits, to prevent making excuses.

Takeaway: Better habits = fewer excuses.

"Ninety-nine percent of the failures come from people who have the habit of making excuses."
— GEORGE WASHINGTON CARVER

My rules and habits are changeable. Nothing is set in stone.

Resistance to change is normal because fear of the unknown is scary. We hesitate because the status quo feels safe. However, if we can identify our resistance and overcome it, rather than viewing change as negative, we can see it as an opportunity for growth.

When change occurs, which it inevitably will, adjust the rules and habits to prevent getting trapped in fears and limiting beliefs. If change is a struggle, start by taking small strides to build resilience. We don't have to do it all at once. The unknown could be a blessing in disguise because it offers us a chance to create something new.

Takeaway: Don't fear change. See it as a chance to evolve.

> "Some rules are nothing but old habits that people are afraid to change."
> — THERESE ANNE FOWLER

BUILD A BETTER DAY FOR SUCCESS

I embrace my self-worth.

Every day is a new opportunity to become the person you desire. Your daily choices shape your future. When you build better habits, you'll receive better results. Elevate your practices and achieve success. Soon, they will become routine and a way of life. Never forget that you have worth, importance, and power.

Takeaway: Are you embracing your greatness?

> "Each day is an opportunity to craft your best life. Each day brings a chance to choose your greatness."
> — ROBIN SHARMA

4

Develop a Growth Mindset

"It would astonish us what we could accomplish if we truly believed in ourselves."

— LYNN LOK-PAYNE

BUILD A BETTER DAY FOR SUCCESS

I will open my mind to see different possibilities.

Do you lean toward a fixed or a growth mindset?

A fixed mindset sees change and improvement as impossible. A person with this mindset won't try. They fear failure and dwell on weaknesses rather than strengths. They often think that this is just the way things are, but there are other potentialities.

A growth mindset focuses on possibilities. People with this mindset actively pursue personal development. If they don't know how to do something, they learn. They take risks, experiment, and find lessons in failure.

A mindset is simply a collection of the beliefs you created, inherited, or picked up. You have the power to change it. Train yourself to focus on growth and opportunities instead of failure and obstacles.

Takeaway: Listen to Roy T. Bennett, "Turn your obstacles into opportunities and your problems into possibilities."

> "You can change your mindset.
> It's up to you to build a better one."
> — LYNN LOK-PAYNE

DEVELOP A GROWTH MINDSET

My definition of winning is my progress.

Society often values winning first place instead of setting personal bests. Focusing on our own growth is more important. While we might not have the capacity to run a mile in four minutes or lift fifty pounds, we can focus on improving upon our previous results. It's not always about the finish line—it's how far we've come from where we started.

Takeaway: Personal growth is the real win.

> "The will to win, the desire to succeed, the urge to reach your full potential...these are the keys that will unlock the door to personal excellence."
> — CONFUCIUS

I am my greatest asset.

Invest in improving yourself for the best returns on success. Be a lifelong student and approach things with a beginner's mind. Masters and experts continuously pursue growth in their crafts.

Takeaway: The ultimate gift is investing in your own personal development.

> "The swiftest way to triple your success is to double your investment in personal development."
> — ROBIN SHARMA

Lifelong learning provides me with the optimal tools for success.

Educating yourself on different topics enhances success. Research has shown that learning or doing something new activates dopamine neurons. This can speed up and optimize the process of gaining knowledge across all areas of your life.[13]

Takeaway: Self-education is key to success.

> "Strengthening skill sets is one thing that a person trying to accomplish any goal should practice."
> — SARFRAZ SOHAIL

Taking action silences my inner critic.

When thoughts of "I can't" appear, challenge them by doing something. Grab a pencil and write one sentence. Pick up a paintbrush and paint a sun. Do a few wall push-ups. Just begin.

Action helps to mute the negative self-talk. Revise destructive narratives with more encouraging words and have an "I can" attitude.

Takeaway: Be proactive.

> "If you hear a voice within you say 'you cannot paint,' then by all means paint, and that voice will be silenced."
> — VINCENT VAN GOGH

I visualize and feel success.

We tend to concentrate on what is missing in our lives and envision worst-case scenarios. However, what we focus on manifests. Envision victory. Think and believe it's possible.

Champions picture themselves making the shot, closing the sale, getting the job, receiving the degree, or mastering the skill. Visualization is a great strategy for achieving success.

Takeaway: If you can see and feel it, you possess the potential to achieve it.

> "If you want to win, visualize yourself winning. People often lose because they concentrate on the wrong things; they focus on what they don't want instead of what they do want."
>
> — LYNN LOK-PAYNE

I am crafting a narrative that's more empowering.

We can get so wrapped up in our stories that we hesitate, quit, or don't even try.

You are the author and the pen is in your hands. Rewrite your narrative and create a greater story. Then get ready for a transformation that will profoundly impact your life.

Building a more powerful storyline is the first step toward personal success.

Takeaway: When you change your story, you change your life.

> "The only thing standing between you and your dream is the story you keep telling yourself as to why you can't achieve it."
> — JORDAN BELFORT

DEVELOP A GROWTH MINDSET

Action matters more than the outcome.

We spend most of our time in the pursuit of the dream, not its realization. Seek fulfillment and joy during the entire process. Savor each moment and welcome everything that comes your way, even the losses because they are essential for growth. Put in the energy. Push forward. Play full out.

Takeaway: Go for it. Don't hold back.

> "You've got to get to the stage in life where going for it is more important than winning or losing."
> — ARTHUR ASHE

BUILD A BETTER DAY FOR SUCCESS

I refuse to let my fears, doubts, and worries block the way to my dreams.

Every successful person has experienced deep uncertainty, and at some point, they weren't fully sure about their next steps. However, they didn't let these concerns stop them. They created a plan, executed it, and reconfigured when necessary. They worked through the doubt because they realized it was crucial to fulfilling their dreams. They knew they had to want it more than their worry.

Face the unknown. When you can embrace the fear, you conquer it. If we had faith in ourselves, we would be amazed at what we could accomplish.

Takeaway: Slay the dragons of fear.

> "The brave man is not he who does not feel afraid, but he who conquers that fear."
> — NELSON MANDELA

Today, I'll focus on the next single task that leads to my goal.

Focusing on one task isn't easy when so much demands our attention. We get overwhelmed with multitasking or distracted by 'the shiny new thing.' I get it. I've been there myself.

Studies have shown that multitasking doesn't work. "It takes time (an average of 15 minutes) to re-orient to a primary task after a distraction such as an email. Efficiency can drop by as much as 40%," according to *Harvard Business Review*.[14] Don't multitask; focus on one thing at a time.

Takeaway: Singular focus results in greater productivity.

> "Focus on the one task that will get the needle moving in the right direction."
> — LYNN LOK-PAYNE

My success is amplified by my focus.

When we have laser-like focus, we enter a flow state that births inspiration, solutions, and new ideas. When we tap into this state, we become completely absorbed in our activity or thoughts, causing distractions to fade away and time to feel like it doesn't exist. It's like we become one with the mission. In other words, it's "being in the zone."

In a flow state, there is no struggle and ideas flow effortlessly. A ten-year study revealed that productivity increases by five times when working in a flow state.[15] It's like being turbocharged. Who wouldn't want that?

Takeaway: Focus enhances productivity.

> "The successful warrior is the average man, with laser-like focus."
>
> — BRUCE LEE

I choose quality over quantity.

I admit it: I used to brag about working 60+ hours a week, like it was a badge of honor. Our society often glorifies the grind. Because time is one of our most valuable resources, it's crucial for us to learn how to work smarter, not harder.

Takeaway: Success is within our reach when we prioritize quality over quantity.

> "We think, mistakenly, that success is the result of the amount of time we put in at work, instead of the quality of time we put in."
> — ARIANNA HUFFINGTON

I may not like the obstacles I'm given, but I can make the most out of them.

Life throws you curve balls when you don't expect it. It's not what happens to you, it's how you react. Don't look at adversity as doom and gloom. Instead, choose to accept it and find a way to move forward. Change your perspective.

By looking at things from a fresh vantage point, better solutions may reveal themselves. Don't lose sight of your goals. Keep your eyes open until you reach home plate.

Takeaway: I can rise above adversity.

> "Things work out best for those who make the best of how things work out."
> — JOHN WOODEN

DEVELOP A GROWTH MINDSET

My success is determined by my perseverance, not my failure.

Failing doesn't mean that you won't succeed. Researchers from the Kellogg School of Management studied awards that were given to young scientists from the National Institutes of Health.[16] These awards averaged more than $1,000,000.

They looked at the winners and near-misses; scientists who were close, but didn't receive the award. Researchers discovered that the near-miss group actually had more 'hit' papers in the top 5% of citations than the scientists who won the awards.

Just because you're not at the top now doesn't mean you won't succeed. Praise and accolades are not always indicative of success.

Takeaway: Persevere because success is not limited to those who receive the acclaim.

> "It doesn't matter how many times you fail. You only have to be right once and then everyone can tell you that you are an overnight success."
> — MARK CUBAN

Mistakes and failures are important directions on the path to success.

Success requires the ability to handle and navigate errors and defeats. The insights we gain from these moments influence our achievements. Failed attempts lead to improvement, whether it's expanding upon an idea, upgrading a product, or increasing self-knowledge.

Takeaway: Embrace failure's lessons as they bring us closer to victory.

> "When we view failure as an excellent teacher, our mindset shifts to reveal the wisdom it offers. This one change can transform our lives and open the door to success."
> — LYNN LOK-PAYNE

DEVELOP A GROWTH MINDSET

I center my efforts on achieving my goals.

What you focus on grows. Instead of dwelling on your failures, you can build confidence by redirecting your attention to your successes. This mindset seeks solutions rather than sticking to the problem. Whatever you obsess over will inevitably multiply. Learn from the losses, move on, and concentrate on your wins.

Takeaway: Develop a mindset that empowers you to take action. It plays a vital role in success.

> "Successful people maintain a positive focus in life no matter what is going on around them. They stay focused on their past successes rather than their past failures, and on the next action steps they need to take to get them closer to the fulfillment of their goals rather than all the other distractions that life presents to them."
> — JACK CANFIELD

I define who I am.

Who is the person you want to be? The answer is yours for the taking. Your daily thoughts, habits, and routines shape your future self. Winning or losing is not predetermined at birth. You get to decide who you are.

Takeaway: When you believe in yourself, you've already won.

> "You were not born a winner, and you were not born a loser. You are what you make yourself to be."
> — LOU HOLTZ

DEVELOP A GROWTH MINDSET

I am the creator of my own opportunities.

Take charge and don't wait for someone else to make the first move. When we put in the work, we are rewarded with choices. Discover a world of possibilities by opening your own door. Trust in your abilities and make it a point to show up for yourself every day. Become the role model of who you want to be. That's when opportunities and synchronicities come rushing in.

Takeaway: You create your own fate by taking action.

> "Some people only ask others to do something. I believe that, why should I wait for someone else? Why don't I take a step and move forward?"
> — MALALA YOUSAFZAI

The best is yet to come.

Develop a growth mindset and embrace new opportunities. Expand your horizons by exploring unfamiliar places and opening new doors. Pursue learning, expand your knowledge, and advance your expertise. Seize adventure and travel far. Do different things. Push forward. Be curious. Be unafraid. Be brave. Be daring. Be bold.

This is not the time to slow down and take a bow, nor is this is the only stage or your final act. There are more roles and curtain calls waiting for you. Keep making progress. Cultivate a mindset that believes the best is yet to come. Because it's true. Your future holds great things and it's there waiting for you to claim it.

Takeaway: Your passport to a new beginning awaits. Begin your journey today.

> "People ask, 'What's the best role you've ever played?' The next one."
> — KEVIN KLINE

5

Don't Give Up

"Success takes time. We need to nurture it
if we want it to grow. Have patience.
What was once a seed eventually becomes a tree."

— LYNN LOK-PAYNE

BUILD A BETTER DAY FOR SUCCESS

I'm not willing to abandon my dreams.

Repeat after me: I won't give up.

Takeaway: Don't quit. Stay strong and keep going.

> "If it's important to you, never give up."
> — LYNN LOK-PAYNE

DON'T GIVE UP

It's possible if I believe.

In the beginning, any project or goal may seem impossible to complete. It can feel too big, unachievable, or overwhelming. However, even your most ambitious dreams can come to life with care, consistency, and resourcefulness.

Look how far you've already come. If you believe, you can achieve.

Takeaway: Belief is the cornerstone of success.

"It always seems impossible until it's done."
— NELSON MANDELA

BUILD A BETTER DAY FOR SUCCESS

Each day I'm getting closer to reaching my goal.

Sometimes we give up out of frustration or we come across another hitch that makes us want to throw in the towel. What if we gave it just one more attempt? We may never realize how close we are to success if we don't give it a shot.

Takeaway: Hang in there.

> "Never give up, for that is just the place and time that the tide will turn."
> — **HARRIET BEECHER STOWE**

Visualize, devise, revise, and optimize.

Visualize your success, develop new plans, make mistakes, change the way you do things, try again, and focus on what works. Don't stop.

Takeaway: Give it another go.

> "Our greatest weakness lies in giving up.
> The most certain way to succeed
> is always to try just one more time."
> — THOMAS EDISON

BUILD A BETTER DAY FOR SUCCESS

I release the fear that stands in the way of my dreams.

Don't give attention to the obstacle. Focus your gaze forward and concentrate on the target. It's like motion sickness; keep your eyes on the horizon and avoid looking sideways. Otherwise, you'll feel off balance. It's the same with your goals; direct your attention to the destination.

Takeaway: Keep your eyes on the goal.

> "Obstacles are those frightful things you see when you take your eyes off your goal."
> — HENRY FORD

DON'T GIVE UP

When I choose to pursue my hopes and dreams, fulfillment follows.

It's easy to let fear guide our choices. The unfamiliar can be scary. However, living this way doesn't make us satisfied. It leaves us feeling empty, like something is missing. It's easy to doubt our dreams and believe they're unattainable. We can't let fear take over and block us from attempting our desires. We must try. Otherwise, we will look back and wish we had.

Stay strong in your dreams. If your desire is greater than your fear, you can overcome and prevail.

Takeaway: Let your heart be your guide.

"May your choices reflect your hopes, not your fears."
— NELSON MANDELA

With hope, I can build the destiny I desire.

Hope, driven by faith, belief, and optimism, is essential for success. We have the power to change our lives and hope gives us the inspiration to see a different future. It brings meaning to our days, supplying us with the imagination and possibilities to design our fate.

Takeaway: Master your fate with hope. Press onward and trust in a positive outcome.

> "Most of the important things in the world have been accomplished by people who have kept on trying when there seemed to be no hope at all."
> — DALE CARNEGIE

DON'T GIVE UP

I honor myself by being patient with my progress.

Just as a plant or tree takes time to grow, so do we. Don't rush the process. Cultivate personal development by attending to it each day. When we give ourselves the space to grow, our roots become stronger. Self-growth is sacred. When you feed and nurture yourself, your soul thrives.

Takeaway: Investing in yourself is the seed to growing a great future. Nourish it daily.

> "Be patient with yourself. Self-growth is tender; it's holy ground. There's no greater investment."
> — STEPHEN COVEY

BUILD A BETTER DAY FOR SUCCESS

With persistence, I will get to my destination.

Some things take time to achieve. It's not how long we take to reach the goal, it's that we eventually arrive. Rushing leads to unnecessary stress, mistakes, and missed knowledge. Faster isn't always better. Just like the tortoise and the hare, slow and steady wins the race.

Takeaway: Continue on the trail at your own pace.

> "It does not matter how slowly you go as long as you do not stop."
> — CONFUCIUS

DON'T GIVE UP

If it isn't working, I'll try another way.

In any endeavor, there are obstacles. Don't let it be the reason you give up. Occasionally, things will not work out, so do something different. Sometimes you have to back up the car to move forward or take an unexpected detour to get to your destination. Who knows, it may be an even better route.

Takeaway: The lesson is to persevere. Keep on trucking.

> "You do what you can for as long as you can, and when you finally can't, you do the next best thing. You back up but you don't give up."
>
> — CHUCK YEAGER

My dreams are worth my time.

Frustration and doubt can set in when dreams don't appear based on your timeline. Be flexible. Try not to become overly attached to a specific deadline or preconceived notions of how it should happen. There may be a different or improved timetable. Delays and setbacks in my first book, *Wake Up! Change Up! Rise Up!* turned out to be a blessing in disguise. Look for a new perspective and adapt as needed. If there is an intense desire living inside of you, don't abandon it. There's a reason it's there.

Takeaway: Be patient and trust the journey.

> "Ask yourself, 'How long am I going to work to make my dreams come true?' I suggest you answer, 'As long as it takes.'"
>
> — JIM ROHN

I am never too old to achieve my dreams.

Age is a barrier only if we believe it is. Don't let your age stop you. Limits on it create a self-defeating mindset. How old we are is a number, not a skill level. Age grants us wisdom and knowledge, increasing the chance for us to fulfill our dreams. The more important question may be, "Are my dreams still important to me?"

Dreams at 20 can differ greatly from those at 60. Evaluate your dreams, drop the ones that are no longer relevant, and stick to the ones that resonate with your soul.

Takeaway: Never let your age deter you from pursuing your dreams.

> "There is no expiration date on a dream unless you make one."
> — LYNN LOK-PAYNE

BUILD A BETTER DAY FOR SUCCESS

I listen to my own inner wisdom over the naysayers.

People's disbelief in your capabilities stems from their own lack of vision or belief in themselves, which they project onto you. Don't listen to them. They aren't standing in your shoes. They have no idea what you're capable of or what's possible for you. Trust in yourself and do what feels right.

Takeaway: You can accomplish anything you set your mind to if you believe you can.

> "There are two types of people
> who will tell you that you cannot make a difference
> in this world: those who are afraid to try
> and those who are afraid you will succeed."
>
> **— RAY GOFORTH**

DON'T GIVE UP

Although there may be challenges on the court, I remain determined to take the shot.

Occasionally, we stumble as we make our way to the basket. Failure is not a bad word or something that we should try to avoid at all costs. It just reveals a correction or change is warranted. Sometimes we get blocked when we try to get to the hoop. It's part of the game.

Embracing missed shots and wrong moves can give us the knowledge that ultimately leads to a better shooting percentage and success rate. Give it another go. You'll eventually sink the ball.

Takeaway: Accept and learn from the defeats because they are the prerequisites to success.

> "I've missed more than 9,000 shots in my career. I've lost almost 300 games. Twenty-six times, I've been trusted to take the game-winning shot and missed. I've failed over and over and over again in my life. And that is why I succeed."
> — MICHAEL JORDAN

Even though my actions didn't work out as I expected, that doesn't mean I failed.

Never, ever describe yourself as a failure. The action failed, not you. The steps you took may not have led to success, but you, as a person, are not a failure. It's crucial that you understand this.

Life is a path of stepping stones, some welcomed and some not. In difficult situations where we make a misstep and slip up, shift the perspective. Look at defeat as a chance to start over again with a cheat sheet on what not to do. Each stone gets us closer to our goal.

Takeaway: Failure just means you're one stepping stone closer to succeeding.

> "Failure is only the opportunity to begin again, this time more intelligently."
> — HENRY FORD

Failure reroutes me in the right direction.

Not everything comes effortlessly. In both succeeding and failing, you'll face challenges and question if you're on the right path. However, you are probably closer to your next win than you think. And if it's important to you, persist.

By overcoming challenges, you improve the process and build confidence in yourself. Don't let obstacles or other people weigh you down. I know you can do it. I believe in you!

Takeaway: Don't let failure stop you. Just redirect.

> "Success and failure share the same path. Failure simply has more detours."
> — LYNN LOK-PAYNE

I celebrate all my wins, big and small.

Acknowledge every accomplishment because they are the building blocks on the path to success. Take a moment to congratulate yourself, whether it's on making the first move, recognizing how far you've come, or finishing the hike. Reaching the top of the mountain takes many small steps, one foot in front of the other. Enjoy the trek and applaud yourself.

Takeaway: You deserve to be celebrated.

> "Talk to yourself about your successes; be sure you are recognizing your own accomplishments, no matter how small they may be."
>
> — RHETT POWER

DON'T GIVE UP

I actively contribute to making the world a better place.

Strength, patience, and passion are three necessary components to making dreams come true. You have the inner strength to deal with difficulties, patience to let things unfold, and passion to get up every day and work on your dreams. This is how you create change.

Takeaway: I can make a difference.

> "Always remember, you have within you the strength, the patience, and the passion to reach for the stars to change the world."
> — HARRIET TUBMAN

I am the author of my life's story, which means that I can design a more powerful narrative.

We are the storytellers of our own lives, the living books we write each day. The questions we should ask ourselves are, "What am I creating?" and "Is this the story I want to tell?"

If we are unhappy with our current story, we have the ability to change, edit, and revise it. Although we can't erase the past, we have the power to redefine our lives and envision a new narrative.

Takeaway: Create a more empowering storyline and become the next chapter of who you are meant to be.

> "We always have the power to write a new ending for ourselves."
> — LYNN LOK-PAYNE

6

The Qualities of Leadership

"A title does not define leadership. A great leader is one who inspires others to do their best."

— LYNN LOK-PAYNE

I am a team player.

Success and leadership involve teamwork. As the saying goes, "There is no 'I' in team." Just as it takes a village to raise a child, it takes a team to run a thriving company or organization.

Successful teamwork relies on a positive outlook, the nurturing of others and their ideas, effective collaboration, clear communication, and openness to change. When we can lead people to want to work together to achieve a common goal, nothing is impossible.

Takeaway: Collaboration is essential for success.

> "My responsibility is getting all my players playing for the name on the front of the jersey, not the one on the back."
> — UNKNOWN

Effective leaders are those who serve the whole.

The hallmark of an influential leader is one that has empathy, passion, purpose, and direction. True leadership is understanding that you lead by making decisions for the good of all, not just yourself. Respect others' opinions and be open to their suggestions. When you walk this path, instead of focusing on acclaim or title, others will naturally gravitate toward you.

Takeaway: When I show up as a leader, I become a leader.

> "A great leader is not position or fame.
> It's being a good human."
> — LYNN LOK-PAYNE

I inspire others to be their best selves.

Recognizing that people are the backbone of any organization is an important characteristic of being a leader. A company is nothing without its personnel. To create great businesses, we must value and cultivate our colleagues' and our own skills.

It's critical to respect and treat others well. People will only be as invested in a company as their leaders are in them. Understanding this vital concept makes for an effective leader.

Takeaway: Model the behavior you wish to see.

> "Good leaders build products. Great leaders build cultures. Good leaders deliver results. Great leaders develop people. Good leaders have vision. Great leaders have values. Good leaders are role models at work. Great leaders are role models in life."
> — ADAM GRANT

THE QUALITIES OF LEADERSHIP

I use positive encouragement to help people recognize their talents.

The essence of true leadership lies in guiding others to reach their highest potential, even if they can't envision it for themselves.

A leader gives people the tools they need to tackle their dreams. It's giving them the space to innovate, respecting their process, and wanting them to succeed. A leader is one who points people in the right direction.

Takeaway: Be the person who shines the light on others.

> "The growth and development of people is the highest calling of leadership."
> — HARVEY FIRESTONE

Approaching situations with empathy helps me excel in collaboration and leadership.

There's no greater gift than believing in others. We all have talents to share, but many times, fear stands in our way. We think we are not worthy, our dreams are impossible, or we're afraid of being judged. All of these can keep our gifts hidden.

When we help people to find confidence in themselves, they can do great things.

Takeaway: An effective leader treats others with empathy, respect, and care, inspiring them to believe in their own potential.

> "Leadership is about empathy. It is about having the ability to relate and connect with people for the purpose of inspiring and empowering their lives."
> — OPRAH WINFREY

THE QUALITIES OF LEADERSHIP

I give my undivided attention when communicating with others.

Here are some tips for making people feel understood:
- Focus on the person.
- Let them speak instead of trying to respond.
- Exhibit kindness.

This will show that their opinions matter, that they matter. Compassionate communication connects people.

Takeaway: Acknowledge others' worth, strength, value, and impact. People will remember how you made them feel seen, heard, and appreciated.

> "I've learned that people will forget what you said, people will forget what you did, but people will never forget how you made them feel."
> — MAYA ANGELOU

I lead by example.

I believe it's our actions, more than our words, that influence how others see us. We can't use friendly and kind words, then be cruel and heartless. Act with respect and as the Golden Rule states, "Treat others as you would want to be treated."

Takeaway: Behavior speaks louder than words.

> "What you do has far greater impact than what you say."
> — STEPHEN COVEY

THE QUALITIES OF LEADERSHIP

A skilled leader seeks advice from trusted advisors.

No one walks this life alone, nor do we have all the answers. It's essential to look to others for help, especially those who have already been down the same road. The insights we receive from mentors and teachers are invaluable.

Education from wise masters comes in many forms: one-on-ones, group sessions, seminars, books, podcasts, and more. Keep asking and you'll gain more knowledge. We achieve the best outcome through collaborative learning.

Takeaway: Seeking wise council guides us to find new solutions.

> "Wise leaders generally have wise counselors because it takes a wise person themselves to distinguish them."
>
> **— DIOGENES**

I consciously select my words and ask purposeful questions to gain clarity.

It's important to know the 'why' behind doing something. However, when reflecting on the past, some research suggests that using objective questions starting with 'what' is more effective.[17] A couple of examples are, "What opportunity did our team miss?" and "What could I have done differently?"

Objective questions propel us forward with logical insights instead of ruminating and getting stuck in the past.

Takeaway: Better questions lead to better results.

> "A leader is someone who asks the right questions."
> — LYNN LOK-PAYNE

THE QUALITIES OF LEADERSHIP

I consider challenges as opportunities for something greater to manifest.

Challenges can create chaos and hardships. I'm not lessening their impact. Sometimes they're very stressful and seem impossible to overcome. We all have challenges in life, but it's what we do with these difficulties that determines who we become. When we shift our perspective and see challenges as chances for improvement, they become more manageable.

If we can accept that there is a purpose or a reason for them, then we won't feel the need to fight so hard to resist the challenges. As Sun Tzu said, "Victory comes from finding opportunities in problems."

Takeaway: A leader's impact is measured by how well they respond to challenges.

> "Impactful leaders seize the day by taking challenges and turning them into opportunities."
> — LYNN LOK-PAYNE

BUILD A BETTER DAY FOR SUCCESS

I choose to be optimistic and to have a resilient attitude.

Attitude is everything. It's easy to be positive when things are going well. However, it's moving through the tough times that builds resilience. The growth you discover by working with setbacks cultivates self-esteem and confidence in your capabilities.

Become the leader people look to during challenges. When you are a role model for success, even in the face of adversity, you show others how to be that, too.

Takeaway: Be confident and expect the best.

> "I think whether you're having setbacks or not, the role of a leader is to always display a winning attitude."
> — COLIN POWELL

THE QUALITIES OF LEADERSHIP

My commitment to my own development has a positive ripple effect on those around me.

To achieve the best outcomes, start by improving yourself, then your organization. When you strengthen your foundation, skills, and inner growth, you become more capable of supporting others in cultivating their abilities. You can't give to others what you don't already have.

Ask, "How can I support my company and its people?" It's never too late to make a change. The organization benefits when individuals are supported in their growth.

Takeaway: Company value starts with you valuing yourself.

> "If you want to improve the organization, you have to improve yourself, and the organization gets pulled up with you."
> — INDRA NOOYI

If I want my life to change, I must first change myself.

Creating change requires developing a deep self-awareness, both externally and internally. External self-awareness is understanding how others perceive you, while internal self-awareness is understanding yourself.

Harvard Business Review identifies four leadership archetypes and reveals that only 10-15% of people are truly self-aware.[18] Determine your position on the chart to enhance your personal growth and become a more effective leader.

THE FOUR SELF-AWARENESS ARCHETYPES[19]

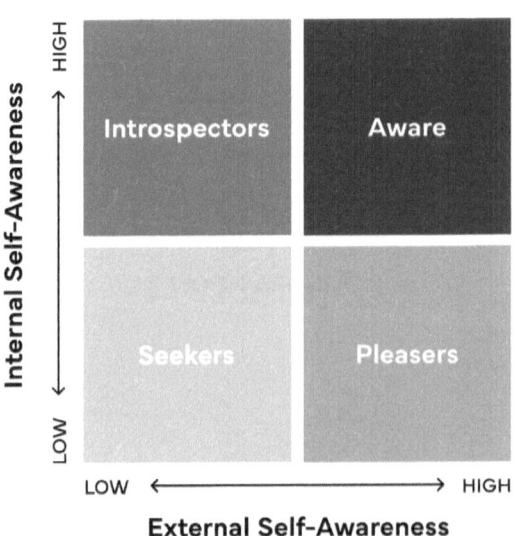

THE QUALITIES OF LEADERSHIP

- Seekers: Low internal and external awareness. These individuals are unaware of their own identity, values, and how they are perceived by their teams. They can feel stuck with their performance or relationships.

- Pleasers: Low internal and high external awareness. This archetype is so fixated on how they come across to others that they may neglect their own priorities. They tend to make choices that aren't in service of their own success and fulfillment.

- Introspectors: High internal and low external awareness. This group is clear on who they are, but don't challenge their own views or get feedback from others. This can harm relationships and limit success.

- Aware: High internal and external awareness. Those in this archetype are confident in their identity, clear on what they want to accomplish, and appreciative of others' constructive thoughts. This is where leaders understand the true advantages of self-awareness.

Takeaway: Self-awareness is linked to improved decision-making, communication, relationships, and leadership.

> "Everyone thinks of changing the world, but no one thinks of changing himself."
> — LEO TOLSTOY

I bring value to the table by improving myself, sharing the knowledge, and helping others succeed.

Add value by improving your skills, investing in personal development, and embracing a growth mindset. Make an impact by sharing what you've learned, showing kindness, and treating people with respect. How can your skills be of service?

Takeaway: Success naturally follows when you share your value.

> "Try not to become a person of success, but rather try to become a person of value."
> — ALBERT EINSTEIN

THE QUALITIES OF LEADERSHIP

Leaders create their own course and set sail on the journey.

You can chart your own path and begin a new voyage. Leaders and innovators dream of what could be. They pioneer innovative ideas, create new concepts, and forge new directions. Leaders carry their passion and excitement into all their endeavors. They don't allow others' doubts to hold them back.

You are the captain of your ship. Steer it in the direction you choose. As Captain Kirk said in Star Trek, "To boldly go where no man has gone before." That's what leaders do. In order to make progress, they brave uncharted territory.

Takeaway: Be a trailblazer and innovate. Embark now!

> "Do not follow where the path may lead.
> Go instead where there is no path and leave a trail."
> — RALPH WALDO EMERSON

7

Dream Big

"When you believe in your dreams, anything is possible."

— LYNN LOK-PAYNE

Happiness is mine for the taking when I follow my dreams.

Dream big. Imagination is the start of any goal. What is it you want to accomplish? How do you want to live? Who do you want to be and why? How do you want to be remembered? What does this all look like? Make a list, figure out what's important to you, and then create the stepping stones to achieve your goals. When you pursue your dreams, you may reveal your purpose.

Time keeps ticking. It doesn't wait for everything to align. Don't let this moment slip away. Go after your goals.

Takeaway: Be an explorer, navigate your desires, and live your dream life.

> "The biggest adventure you can take is to live the life of your dreams."
> — OPRAH WINFREY

DREAM BIG

I believe in my dreams.

Dreams require fuel to propel forward, just like a car. And the fuel for dreams is belief—in yourself, your ideas, and the possibilities.

Along the road, you'll hit potholes and make wrong turns. Traffic jams and delays will unfold because your conviction needs to be serviced. And you may even run out of gas once in a while. That's okay. It's all part of the journey. Just refuel with hope, faith, and trust.

You're doing great, keep moving forward. You're on the right track. Dream. Believe. Achieve. Receive.

Takeaway: Trust that you have what it takes to accomplish your dreams.

> "The future belongs to those who believe in the beauty of their dreams."
> **— ELEANOR ROOSEVELT**

Every day I close the gap between me and the realization of my dream.

Ask yourself if what you're doing today is moving you closer or farther from your dream. It's easy to get distracted or bogged down by life's daily tasks. But at what point do you stop putting off your dreams and happiness?

Make it a daily practice to visualize your dreams and actively go after what brings you joy. Act with boldness, bravery, and confidence. Life is one grand adventure, so make the most of every day. *Are you in?*

Takeaway: Any day you move toward your happiness, you help bring your dreams to life.

> "Even if you can't just snap your fingers
> and make a dream come true, you can travel
> in the direction of your dream, every single day
> and you can shorten the distance
> between the two of you."
> — DOUGLAS PAGELS

When I believe in myself, I can do the unimaginable.

Taking small measures daily will help us accomplish our dreams. It's like going up a ladder. Each rung brings us closer to the top. Advancing to the next level requires us to step up. What can we do today to make progress? No action is too small. Each one brings us closer to our goal.

Takeaway: Climb and ascend to a brand-new future.

> "What you have done is nothing compared to what you can do."
> — GRANT CARDONE

I can feel safe when I venture into new experiences.

Dreams require a vital element: imagination. Instead of focusing on what is, imagine what could be. This might mean the dream is something beyond our current reality. Just remember what was once fantasy, like cell phones or electric cars, are now everyday items.

Takeaway: Open your mind and envision new possibilities.

> "Today's accomplishments were yesterday's impossibilities."
> — ROBERT H. SCHULLER

DREAM BIG

My imagination is the starting point to my next success.

Tap into the imaginative power within you and unlock your creativity. Rediscover your inner child, the one who could create castles out of sand or make rocket ships out of boxes. Let imagination be your muse and allow it to take you wherever it desires. Have fun, loosen up, and be silly. Success begins with a dream that's fueled by imagination. Go with it and enjoy the ride.

Takeaway: Let your imagination guide you in fulfilling your wildest dreams.

> "All the breaks you need in life
> wait within your imagination.
> Imagination is the workshop of your mind,
> capable of turning mind energy
> into accomplishment and wealth."
>
> — NAPOLEON HILL

BUILD A BETTER DAY FOR SUCCESS

I'm confident in my ability to manifest my own opportunities.

It takes courage to chase dreams, especially when the world says you can't. This is the point where some people throw in the towel. They listen to the doubters and critics instead of believing in themselves. Or they accept the little (and sometimes big) internal voice telling them it's not possible. Tune it out.

By having confidence in your dreams, you will find hope, bravery, and belief. Be courageous and trust in your abilities. The game changer is you!

Takeaway: Believe in your power to achieve personal success.

> "Don't be in the business of playing it safe.
> Be in the business of creating possibilities for greatness."
> — ROBERT IGER

DREAM BIG

I am the architect of my life and have the courage to shape my future.

Walt Disney serves as a great model for pursuing dreams and taking risks rather than playing it safe. He was fired from his first animation job because he "lacked imagination and had no good ideas."[20] He faced bankruptcy, had a nervous breakdown, and failed at acting.[21] He lost the rights to his first big success, Oswald the Lucky Rabbit, experienced striking animators, and 300 bankers turned him down for loans.[22] These are just a few of the challenges he encountered.

Despite the odds, he chased his imagination, persisted through difficulties, and dared to take risks. Now it's nearly impossible to picture a world without Disney. Walt's life is a reminder for us to not give up, believe in our dreams, build our own paths, know that curiosity births creativity, and love what we do.

Takeaway: Dare to dream and find the courage to bring those dreams to life.

> "All our dreams can come true,
> if we have the courage to pursue them."
> — WALT DISNEY

Destiny is guided by my dreams. What do I want to create?

Dreams and inspiration are the voices of our inner guidance system, pointing us in the direction of change and new creations. Once we elevate our thoughts and beliefs, we allow more opportunities to present themselves.

When we have the determination to achieve what we truly desire, our destiny becomes clear.

Takeaway: Your destiny awaits!

> "Don't downgrade your dream just to fit your reality. Upgrade your conviction to match your destiny."
> — STUART SCOTT

I hold the key to my future.

Our purpose is to discover and live out our dreams. We are meant to work toward our desires even if the world thinks we can't reach them. People with big dreams simply don't follow the crowd. They push boundaries, innovate, and forge new ideas.

Takeaway: Stand out by creating a future that is uniquely yours.

> "Don't conform yourself to the world.
> Dream big and design your own path."
> — LYNN LOK-PAYNE

BUILD A BETTER DAY FOR SUCCESS

I will focus on the guidance from people who have already achieved my desired results.

I believe dreams are only given to us if they are possible. This doesn't mean we should share them with everyone. Choose wisely. Some people may lack the ability to imagine your dreams succeeding. That's alright. Not everyone has to believe. Seek those who can see your vision.

It's important to follow your happiness. And even when no one else believes, you must persist. Your dream is a reason you are here.

Takeaway: Only share your dreams with those who can believe.

"Stop telling your big dreams to small-minded people."
— STEVE HARVEY

… DREAM BIG

I choose to follow my own dreams.

Happiness comes when you chase your dreams, not from pleasing others. Your parents, peers, family, or friends may have different opinions on what you should do. Trust your own instincts instead of blindly following their advice. If you ignore your inner wisdom and pursue what others want for you, you may experience frustration, regret, or misery.

Chasing what sets your soul on fire leads to fulfillment, happiness, and peace. Where does your passion and joy live? That's where you will find success.

Takeaway: Seek what you desire, not what others desire for you.

> "People suffer when they pursue a life or chase a dream that doesn't belong to them."
> — CAROLINE MYSS

My dreams lead me to the knowledge I need to succeed.

Facts of our current reality are important; however, dreams fuel the creativity and unconventional thinking necessary for innovation. Relying only on data may prevent new ideas from emerging. Many groundbreaking concepts start as a dream, a 'what-if.'

If we feel deeply about something, we must persevere. Otherwise, we may never find out what's truly possible.

Takeaway: Creativity and innovation are the keys to unlocking your potential.

> "Never give up on what you really want to do. The person with big dreams is more powerful than the one with all the facts."
> — ALBERT EINSTEIN

DREAM BIG

My dreams are destined to become a reality when they are backed by my determination.

As the saying goes, "Where there is a will, there is a way."

Takeaway: Seize your destiny!

> "So many of our dreams at first seem impossible, then they seem improbable, and then, when we summon the will, they soon become inevitable."
> — CHRISTOPHER REEVE

BUILD A BETTER DAY FOR SUCCESS

There are no limits in manifesting my desires, no matter how big.

Small dreams lead to minor success. Big dreams bring colossal success. Both require effort and are equally important. If a big dream seems too daunting, break it down into manageable daily actions. The path to the top involves walking up the staircase, one stair at a time.

Don't be afraid to dream big. Dig deep, unleash your potential, and fulfill your dreams.

Takeaway: Why dream small when I can dream big?

> "I always say, 'To have a big dream requires the same effort as having a small dream. Dream big!'"
> — JORGE PAULO LEMANN

I accept the obstacles and won't let them prevent me from achieving my dreams.

Ambitious dreams inspire us to achieve something beyond our expectations. They motivate us to overcome challenges by emphasizing the value of the outcome over the pain of leaving our comfort zones. With any dream, there will be difficulties. Big dreams often have more hurdles than smaller ones, yet they can also have greater rewards and this keeps us motivated to continue.

Takeaway: Succeed in your endeavors by overcoming obstacles.

> "Big dreams drive us to do things we'd never do for lesser dreams — in many ways they almost pull us through the obstacles we're likely to have on the way to reaching them."
> — VIC JOHNSON

Believing in possibility attracts the right people and knowledge for my success.

When we act upon our dreams, the universe meets us halfway with coincidence, chance, serendipity, and fate. Often, it's even closer than that. When we make the effort, we attract blessings and opportunities.

Takeaway: Your dreams are waiting for you. Seize them now.

> "When you want something, all the universe conspires in helping you to achieve it."
> — PAULO COELHO

8

Live Your Legacy

"Start living your legacy. Focus on doing things that bring you joy and act with compassion every day for others and yourself."

— LYNN LOK-PAYNE

BUILD A BETTER DAY FOR SUCCESS

The pursuit of inner peace and joy is my definition of success.

Many times, when we think of success, we think about external things, like houses, cars, awards, or titles. Yet the most valuable successes are internal—happiness, contentment, self-worth, serenity, and love. You can't put a value on inner peace; it's priceless.

When these values become our top priorities, we align with our truest selves and find a sense of wholeness, joy, and contentment.

Takeaway: Define success based on your values.

> "Success? I don't know what that word means. I'm happy. But success, that goes back to what in somebody's eyes success means. For me, success is inner peace. That's a good day for me."
>
> — DENZEL WASHINGTON

LIVE YOUR LEGACY

I make intentional choices to live a life of no regrets.

Palliative care nurse, Bronnie Ware, who worked with people during their last weeks of life, wrote *The Top Five Regrets of Dying*. The biggest regret was living life based on others' expectations rather than embracing their true selves. The remaining four regrets included wishing they hadn't worked so hard, not having the courage to express their feelings, losing touch with friends, and not allowing themselves to be happier.[23]

Happiness is a choice. Do things that make you happy. Don't let your job consume your life. Speak your truth and stop worrying about what others think. Stay in touch with people you care about. Have fun, laugh more, love deeper.

Takeaway: Let "living with no regrets" be your personal mission statement or motto.

> "A friend of mine said something powerful at his grandfather's funeral. He said that the greatest lesson from his grandfather's life was that he died empty, because he accomplished everything he wanted, with no regrets. I think that, along with leaving a legacy, would be the greatest sign of success."
>
> — MARVIN SAPP

BUILD A BETTER DAY FOR SUCCESS

I consciously choose to use my time wisely and surround myself with uplifting people.

Pay attention to how you spend your day and be productive in the areas that really count. Find your tribe. Surround yourself with people who get you and minimize your interactions with those who don't. Otherwise, you'll waste energy trying to make them understand your choices and dreams. Devote yourself to what resonates in your heart. It's your life. Live it on your terms.

Takeaway: Invest your time in what matters most to you.

> "Our legacy is how we spend our time and who we spend it with."
>
> — JIM STENGEL

LIVE YOUR LEGACY

I am making my life count.

Live with zest and enthusiasm. Travel and take new adventures, linger in nature, create meaningful memories with loved ones, and carve out time to do activities you love. Cherish the small moments, like watching a sunrise or having coffee with a friend, as they can be our most treasured. Make your moments count.

We don't know how much time is left, so make it worthwhile. As Maya Angelou magnificently said, "Make a mark on the world that can't be erased." And that she did.

Takeaway: Design a life including joyful experiences that people will remember.

> "Life is not measured by the number of breaths we take, but by the moments that take our breath away."
> — MAYA ANGELOU

I am mindful of choosing options that are good for the earth.

Are we being good stewards in preserving the environment? Our actions leave footprints that affect the planet. Ask, "What step can I take today to ensure a brighter future?" Actions do speak louder than words.

Takeaway: One of the greatest gifts we can give to future generations is leaving the world a better place.

> "We don't inherit the earth from our ancestors, we borrow it from our children."
> — DAVID BROWER

LIVE YOUR LEGACY

I strive to leave a positive impact on the people I meet.

Most of us will not create earth-shattering discoveries, however, we can positively influence the lives of others in our community by being good humans. Be thoughtful, caring, compassionate, and appreciative. That is how we change the world. Affecting one life at a time.

Takeaway: Being kind leaves a lasting impression.

> "We might not be the ones to change the world.
> We might not belong to the few that 'put a ding in the universe.' We might not be something the whole world would celebrate.
> But...in the little corners that we live;
> in the lives that we've played a part in,
> we should be nothing but unforgettable."
> — NESTA JOJOE ERSKINE

My intention is to make the people in my life feel important, heard, and understood.

If someone can say that they're a better person because you were in their life, that's true success. By letting others know their value, you can make a difference in their well-being. This will come back to you in wonderful and unexpected ways.

Start your day off right by doing good deeds with love and intention. Now, that's what I call a meaningful and noble life.

Takeaway: Become the person others look up to.

> "The mark you leave on every soul becomes your legacy. Your goal should be to leave people feeling better than they did before they met you."
>
> — LYNN LOK-PAYNE

I want people to remember me in their hearts.

I believe being of good character is the best legacy. Character comes from the Greek word *kharaktēr* meaning "engraved mark," or "symbol or imprint on the soul."[24]

Leave your imprint by being kind, generous, compassionate, open, understanding, honest, loyal, and reliable with a strong moral compass. Let go and forgive. When you cultivate these qualities, you leave an unforgettable mark in people's hearts.

Takeaway: Let your heart serve as your compass for life.

> "Carve your name on hearts, not tombstones. A legacy is etched into the minds of others and the stories they share about you."
> — SHANNON L. ADLER

Today, I make it my mission to spread joy and kindness to everyone I meet.

We are all interconnected in this tapestry of life. No one comes into this world alone. Our lives and stories are intertwined.

Have empathy, contribute, and add value wherever you go. Don't worry so much about leaving behind monetary riches. Instead, spark joy and see the goodness in people. This is what they will remember.

The secret to a life well-lived lies in forming meaningful connections.

Takeaway: Make the most out of today and leave a lasting impression.

> "Each morning we are born again.
> What we do today is what matters most."
> — BUDDHA

LIVE YOUR LEGACY

I'm truly embracing and enjoying life.

We all want to feel that our lives are significant, that they have purpose and meaning. We need to know that we mattered. Our time on this earth is limited, so make it count. No grand gesture is required. It's just about showing up every day to follow your dreams, spread love, be kind, be happy, and just be you.

Takeaway: Making the world a little better because you were here is the best legacy.

> "In the end, it's not the years in your life that count. It's the life in your years."
>
> — UNKNOWN

Playlist for Success

- "Better Days" by Goo Goo Dolls
- "Happy" by Pharrell Williams
- "Have It All" by Jason Mraz
- "Golden" by Jill Scott
- "Best Day of My Life" by American Authors
- "What a Feeling" by Irene Cara
- "Rise Up" by Andra Day
- "Unwritten" by Natasha Bedingfield
- "Don't Stop Belivin'" by Journey
- "Over the Rainbow" by Israel Kamakawiwo'ole
- "Brand New Day" by Van Morrison
- "Good Day" by Brett Eldredge
- "Don't Blink" by Kenny Chesney
- "Runnin' Down a Dream" by Tom Petty
- "Better Days" by Le'Andria Johnson
- "What a Wonderful World" by Louis Armstrong

Thank You

I want to express my gratitude to all the readers, listeners, and personal growth enthusiasts who have been with me throughout this journey. I am forever grateful!

If you enjoyed this book, please take a few moments to leave a review or star rating on Amazon, Barnes & Noble, Goodreads, or wherever you hang out. I really appreciate it!

Notes

CHAPTER 2: CREATE GOALS

1. "Smart Goals: A How To Guide," *University of California, Office of The President*, 2016, https://www.ucop.edu/local-human-resources/_files/performance-appraisal/How%20to%20write%20SMART%20Goals%20v2.pdf.
2. "Introducing the Eisenhower Matrix," *Eisenhower.Me*, Accessed April 1, 2024, https://www.eisenhower.me/eisenhower-matrix.
3. Ibid.

CHAPTER 3: BUILD BETTER HABITS

4. Society for Personality and Social Psychology, "How We Form Habits, Change Existing Ones," *Science Daily*, August 8, 2014, https://www.sciencedaily.com/releases/2014/08/140808111931.htm.
5. Charles Duhigg, "Habits: How They Form and How To Break Them," By Terry Gross, Fresh Air, *NPR*, March 5, 2012, https://www.npr.org/2012/03/05/147192599/habits-how-they-form-and-how-to-break-them.
6. James Clear, "How To Start New Habits That Actually Stick," *James Clear*, Accessed September 12, 2023, https://www.jamesclear.com/three-steps-habit-change.

7. Susan Weinschenk Ph.D., "Shopping, Dopamine, and Anticipation," *Psychology Today*, October 22, 2015, https://www.psychologytoday.com/us/blog/brain-wise/201510/shopping-dopamine-and-anticipation.
8. BJ Fong, "Tiny Habits Recipe Card Template," *Tiny Habits*, Accessed October 4, 2023, https://www.tinyhabits.com/wp-content/uploads/2020/10/tinyhabits-recipe-cards.pdf.
9. Ibid.
10. Morgan Smith, "3 Morning Habits to Help You Be Happier and More Productive at Work, according to Psychologists," *CNBC*, December 19, 2022, https://www.cnbc.com/2022/12/18/psychologists-morning-habits-to-help-you-be-happier-more-productive.html.
11. James Clear, "How Long Does It Take To Actually Form a New Habit?" *James Clear*, Accessed September 12, 2023, https://www.jamesclear.com/new-habit.
12. "Breaking Bad Habits: Why It's So Hard to Change," *National Institute of Health, News In Health*, January 2012, https://newsinhealth.nih.gov/2012/01/breaking-bad-habits#:~:text=Another%20thing%20that%20makes%20habits,and%20suppress%20the%20original%20one.
13. VIB (the Flanders Institute for Biotechnology), "Novelty Speeds Up Learning Thanks to Dopamine Activation," *Science Daily*, February 5, 2020, https://www.sciencedaily.com/releases/2020/02/200205132255.htm.

NOTES

14. Paul Atchley, "You Can't Multitask, So Stop Trying," *Harvard Business Review*, December 21, 2010, https://www.hbr.org/2010/12/you-cant-multi-task-so-stop-tr.
15. Steven Kotler, "Create a Work Environment That Fosters Flow," *Harvard Business Review*, May 6, 2014, Updated October 11, 2019, https://www.hbr.org/2014/05/create-a-work-environment-that-fosters-flow.
16. Jessica Stillman, "Early failure Makes You More Likely to Succeed in the Future, Not Less" *Inc.*, November 1, 2019, https://www.inc.com/jessica-stillman/new-study-early-failure-makes-you-more-likely-to-succeed-in-future-not-less.html.

CHAPTER 6: THE QUALITIES OF LEADERSHIP

17. Tasha Eurich, "What Self-Awareness Really Is (and How to Cultivate It)," *Harvard Business Review*, January 4, 2018, https://www.hbr.org/2018/01/what-self-awareness-really-is-and-how-to-cultivate-it.
18. Ibid.
19. Ibid.

CHAPTER 7: DREAM BIG

20. Rachel Gillett, "How Walt Disney, Oprah Winfrey, and 19 Other Successful People Rebounded After Getting Fired," *Inc.*, October 7, 2015, https://www.

inc.com/business-insider/21-successful-people-who-rebounded-after-getting-fired.html.
21. James Asquith, "Did You Know Walt Disney Was Rejected 300 Times For His Mouse And Theme Park," *Forbes*, December 29, 2019, https://www.forbes.com/sites/jamesasquith/2020/12/29/did-you-know-walt-disney-was-rejected-300-times-for-mickey-mouse-and-his-theme-park.
22. Nic Faitos, "Learning from Our Past Failures," *Forbes*, December 30, 2020, https://www.forbes.com/councils/forbesbusinesscouncil/2021/12/30/learning-from-our-past-failures.

CHAPTER 8: LIVE YOUR LEGACY

23. Bronnie Ware, "The Top Five Regrets of Dying – A Life Transformed by the Dearly Departing," *Bronnie Ware*, Accessed October 19, 2023, https://www.bronnieware.com/regrets-of-the-dying.
24. *Online Etymology Dictionary*, s.v. "Character," Accessed September 12, 2023, https://www.etymonline.com/word/character.

Index

CHAPTER 1: SUCCESS STARTS HERE

I have the power to make my dreams a reality. 2
I can do this! 3
I have faith in myself. 4
I will begin now. 5
If they can do it, then I can, too. 6
I release the beliefs that no longer serve me. 7
What I need to succeed will appear once I start. 8
Today is the day I get into the game! 9
Now is the time for me to act. 10
I trust that my intuition will lead the way. 11
I visualize my success every day. 12
It's up to me to change my life. 13
What am I waiting for? 14
I won't allow my mind's rumination to control my life. 15
Taking small steps will help me reach my dreams. 16
My motivation increases when I honor all of my wins. ...17

CHAPTER 2: CREATE GOALS

I set goals that align with my dreams. 20
I have unlimited potential and endless possibilities. 21

I devise a game plan for my success.................................22
My desire is the foundation of my inspiration.................23
I can reverse engineer my dream life. 24
Action is necessary to achieve my dreams.......................25
I can reach my goals by breaking them down into manageable steps. 26
My goals create the target for my success. 27
Every day I show up for myself and dedicate my time to doing what is necessary. 28
I set realistic goals that challenge and engage me.............29
Understanding my 'why' gives me the purpose to pursue my goals. 30
When I establish a timeline, I can reach my dreams........32
My focus is not just on the end goal, but also on my own growth journey. 33
Commitment to my goal is paramount to success...........34
I concentrate on my own goals, not on what others are thinking or doing. 35
I follow my own desires and dreams. 36
Success is living my purpose. 37
I am more driven to keep going when I align my passions with my purpose..38
I design my destiny..39
I am aware of the power within me................................40
I adapt to achieve my goal. 41
I prioritize the important tasks and delegate or delete the rest. 42
I am in charge of my life...44
I release my limiting beliefs and embrace possibility........45

INDEX

I can achieve my goals when I commit to the work.........46

CHAPTER 3: BUILD BETTER HABITS

My success depends on my daily habits. 50
I am in control of my day. 51
I will replace my bad habits by creating more empowering ones...52
I am mindful of how I allocate my time...........................53
I can build new habits by noticing my daily patterns. 54
Each day, I have the opportunity to change my life through my actions. 55
When I stack my habits, implementing new practices becomes easier. 56
My morning habits create the groundwork for my day. 58
I align my habits to be in sync with my dreams and goals. 59
I practice habits that lead me in the right direction. 60
With small steps, I can transform my habits. 61
When I know the reason and emotion behind a habit, it becomes easier to change. 62
I will step into my power by choosing to uplift my thoughts. 63
I will find a reason to be grateful every day. 64
Today, I stop making excuses and begin working on my dreams..65
I refuse to let my excuses prevent me from achieving my goals. 66

My rules and habits are changeable. Nothing is set in stone. 67
I embrace my self-worth. 68

CHAPTER 4: DEVELOP A GROWTH MINDSET

I will open my mind to see different possibilities. 72
My definition of winning is my progress. 73
I am my greatest asset. 74
Lifelong learning provides me with the optimal tools for success. 75
Taking action silences my inner critic. 76
I visualize and feel success. 77
I am crafting a narrative that's more empowering. 78
Action matters more than the outcome. 79
I refuse to let my fears, doubts, and worries block the way to my dreams. 80
Today, I'll focus on the next single task that leads to my goal. 81
My success is amplified by my focus. 82
I choose quality over quantity. 83
I may not like the obstacles I'm given, but I can make the most out of them. 84
My success is determined by my perseverance, not my failure. 85
Mistakes and failures are important directions on the path to success. 86
I center my efforts on achieving my goals. 87
I define who I am. 88

INDEX

I am the creator of my own opportunities.................89
The best is yet to come....................................90

CHAPTER 5: DON'T GIVE UP

I'm not willing to abandon my dreams. 94
It's possible if I believe. 95
Each day I'm getting closer to reaching my goal.........96
Visualize, devise, revise, and optimize. 97
I release the fear that stands in the way of my dreams. 98
When I choose to pursue my hopes and dreams, fulfillment follows. 99
With hope, I can build the destiny I desire. 100
I honor myself by being patient with my progress.........101
With persistence, I will get to my destination. 102
If it isn't working, I'll try another way. 103
My dreams are worth my time...............................104
I am never too old to achieve my dreams. 105
I listen to my own inner wisdom over the naysayers......106
Although there may be challenges on the court, I remain determined to take the shot. 107
Even though my actions didn't work out as I expected, that doesn't mean I failed. 108
Failure reroutes me in the right direction. 109
I celebrate all my wins, big and small......................110
I actively contribute to making the world a better place. 111
I am the author of my life's story, which means that I can design a more powerful narrative. 112

CHAPTER 6: THE QUALITIES OF LEADERSHIP

I am a team player. 116
Effective leaders are those who serve the whole. 117
I inspire others to be their best selves. 118
I use positive encouragement to help people recognize their talents. 119
Approaching situations with empathy helps me excel in collaboration and leadership. 120
I give my undivided attention when communicating with others. 121
I lead by example. 122
A skilled leader seeks advice from trusted advisors. 123
I consciously select my words and ask purposeful questions to gain clarity. 124
I consider challenges as opportunities for something greater to manifest. 125
I choose to be optimistic and to have a resilient attitude. 126
My commitment to my own development has a positive ripple effect on those around me. 127
If I want my life to change, I must first change myself. 128
I bring value to the table by improving myself, sharing the knowledge, and helping others succeed. 130
Leaders create their own course and set sail on the journey. 131

INDEX

CHAPTER 7: DREAM BIG

Happiness is mine for the taking when I follow my dreams. 134
I believe in my dreams. 135
Every day I close the gap between me and the realization of my dream. 136
When I believe in myself, I can do the unimaginable. 137
I can feel safe when I venture into new experiences. 138
My imagination is the starting point to my next success. 139
I'm confident in my ability to manifest my own opportunities. 140
I am the architect of my life and have the courage to shape my future. 141
Destiny is guided by my dreams. What do I want to create? 142
I hold the key to my future. 143
I will focus on the guidance from people who have already achieved my desired results. 144
I choose to follow my own dreams. 145
My dreams lead me to the knowledge I need to succeed. 146
My dreams are destined to become a reality when they are backed by my determination. 147
There are no limits in manifesting my desires, no matter how big. 148
I accept the obstacles and won't let them prevent me from achieving my dreams. 149

Believing in possibility attracts the right people and knowledge for my success. 150

CHAPTER 8: LIVE YOUR LEGACY

The pursuit of inner peace and joy is my definition of success. 154
I make intentional choices to live a life of no regrets. 155
I consciously choose to use my time wisely and surround myself with uplifting people. 156
I am making my life count. 157
I am mindful of choosing options that are good for the earth. 158
I strive to leave a positive impact on the people I meet. 159
My intention is to make the people in my life feel important, heard, and understood. 160
I want people to remember me in their hearts. 161
Today, I make it my mission to spread joy and kindness to everyone I meet. 162
I'm truly embracing and enjoying life. 163

About the Author

LYNN LOK-PAYNE is the award-winning author of *Wake Up! Change Up! Rise Up!: Practical Tools for Personal Transformation*, which won the prestigious IBPA Book Award, and *Speak This Not That: Positive Affirmations to Have a Better Day*.

As a former CEO and founder of a multi-million-dollar business turned author, Lynn motivates others to become the next chapter of who they are meant to be by creating a more empowering narrative for their life. When not writing, she can be found curled up with a good book, traveling to new locales, and attending concerts.

CONNECT ONLINE
Social Media: @LynnLokPayne
Books and Website: www.LynnLokPayne.com

More From
Lynn Lok-Payne

WELLMINDED MEDIA

CONNECT ONLINE

Follow @LynnLokPayne

Claim a free gratitude guide and more life tools at: LynnLokPayne.com

www.ingramcontent.com/pod-product-compliance
Lightning Source LLC
Chambersburg PA
CBHW060605080526
44585CB00013B/688